MW00328126

love
more

50+ ways to build joy
into childhood

S h a n n o n   L o u c k s

Love More: 50+ ways to build joy into childhood

Copyright © 2019 by Shannon Loucks

All rights reserved. No part of this publication may be reproduced, stored in a retrieval system, or transmitted, in any form or by any means, without the prior written permission of the publisher.

ISBN: 978-1-989499-02-3 (paperback)
ISBN: 978-1-989499-01-6 (ebook)

Cover and Interior Design by JD Smith

Published worldwide by Forever Curious Press
Erin, Ontario, Canada
forevercuriouspress.com

Dedicated to my mother-in-law
Doreen Loucks, for teaching me the
power of unconditional love.

Contents

Introduction

Welcome!

Please jump in.

This book is designed in a flip and read style. It's not required to read from cover to cover. Yet, at the same time, it completely can be. The goal was to create the sort of book you could flip open and discover that one perfect action to insert an extra dose of love into your parenting day.

The book is broken up into two basic sections with all sorts of overlap. Love in action leans toward the sort of things you can do to help infuse joy throughout your child's day. Love in presence leans more toward how you show up for your child throughout your relationship together.

I hope you find at least one thing that sparks your heart and leads to deeper joy for you and your child on this amazing parenting journey.

Letter of Permission

This is your letter of permission to go ahead and simply love your children. Put down those expectations that are ingrained in someone else's idea of what it means to be successful in the world and stare a few moments longer into the precious eyes of the child who stands before you.

Instead of asking how their day was, enquire about what lights their passion, what made them smile today, and what was one place they would like a do over.

Institute a random dance party in the middle of the grocery store in the second before a meltdown threatens to take you all to a place you'd rather not visit. It's okay if everyone turns and looks at you because you're making memories and we could all use more of the happy sort in this lifetime. Say "I love you" over and over again. Not just in words but in the foods you put before them at dinner time or the extra marshmallow on the hot chocolate. Listen more and talk less with the sort of full attention you pay to the most important conversations you have because they are just that: the most important moments of truly getting to know who your child is.

Touch more in cuddles and tickles and wrestling matches. Especially the bigger ones who are making their way farther out into the world so they can always remember your arms are a safe haven.

Undo the places where you were done wrong, so you don't accidentally pass them along to the most precious person you've had the honor to know in this world.

Laugh from the bottom of your belly as you sit side by side on the couch watching the movie you swore had no value but your child was dying to see. Hold in the breath that longs to pull it apart and choose instead to see it through the eyes of wonder that are your child's.

Each day, find one, just one, simple way to love more that being that is your child. It's life's most precious work. I promise.

LOVE IN ACTION

Happy Face Condiments

When you are making a sandwich or toast for your dear one, why not throw down a condiment happy face? I used heart shapes with the mustard every time I made my son a ham and cheese sandwich. Someone said to me once, "But he's not even going to see it."

"That doesn't matter," I explained, "This simple act has me putting a little extra love in the sandwich."

And I think it is true whether the peanut butter and jam on the toast match up to be a mustached bandit or the mayo forms a never-to-be-seen heart. The intention of putting together food with love instead of obligation creates an entirely different experience, for me and for my child, in the moments he catches a glimpse. I dare you to put a heart shaped anything on a sandwich and feel grumpy about making it!

Grocery Store Surprises

I have always been the primary grocery store shopper in this house. It can be viewed as a dull task by some, but one spin I have added is searching for those items that will delight members of my family. The one green apple in the bag of all reds for the person who only likes green apples. The best-loved chocolate bar that is bound to bring a smile to someone's face. The one ingredient that signals a favorite meal is soon to appear. These things put a smile on my face as I pick them up, lightening the load of grocery shopping. A side effect I had not anticipated is it has led to people greeting me at the car each time I arrive home to help unload and unpack the bags. There is joy in looking for those signs of love tucked beneath the bunch of broccoli.

Dance Break

Take a dance break with your child. You don't need to have any special training or moves for this one—you just need to move to the music. We dance a great deal around here. Sometimes I do it to catch a laugh in the strangest of situations. Nothing stops a meltdown midway faster than mom dancing down the cereal aisle (it's worth noting that timing does matter on this one because not every meltdown is conducive to the insertion of humor). Days on end of rain or cold or sickness can be transformed (if only for a few moments) by a stereo turned a couple notches too high and getting your groove on. Play your favorite song while stuck in traffic; turn it up and car dance!

Sing to the Radio

Sing when your favorite songs come on.

Sing about the dishes.

Sing about the clean up that needs to happen.

Singing invites in joy, moves emotion and almost always elevates the mood. The boys and I sing all the time. When they were younger, I could have been accused of singing their entire day to them. The result though is they both sing with wild abandon, like they are alone in the shower, no matter who is listening.

Stick a Candle in It

This idea is inspired by my friend Patti Digh who carries celebration candles with her everywhere and hands them out at events she creates. There is nothing more magical than celebrating the tiny moments in our lives. There is always a reason to celebrate. Even if it boils down to something as simple as "It's Tuesday." Taking the time to notice the little moments we have with our children brings awareness to the right now. And in this moment, with candlelight between us, it's a challenge to think that anything is more important than loving this human being.

Carry Bubbles

Carrying one of those small travel size bubble containers in your purse can cheer up or add to any given moment. Who doesn't love a good sprinkling of bubbles? For me, the bubbles were often just as soothing, or even more soothing, than they were for my child.

Pause. Breath. Blow. Pop. Repeat.

Bubbles are just one example of the tricks you can have tucked away inside of your purse. That's why us moms are ending up with back and shoulder pain: we are literally carrying a bag of tricks with us as we commit to showing up for our children. Throughout my time with my boys my purse has been home to bubbles, crayons, paper, band-aids, rescue remedy, Lego mini figures, coloring books, blank paper, a favorite story, and a phone loaded with new surprise apps in folders labelled with each child's name. I'm armed and ready to dispense joy in any given situation.

Cuddle Wake Up

My youngest still calls out my name when he wakes up each morning. He then flips over to pretend he is asleep so I can cuddle right up next to him and he can wake up to mama cuddles. If you think of all the different ways we have to wake a person up, being cuddled awake is one of the most gentle, loving acts we can offer. Even if your morning is all rushing about and you need to get out the door ten minutes ago, pausing long enough for a little cuddle can help set the tone for the day.

As a side note, other soft and gentle ways that can make waking up to someone else's schedule easier include: tilting the blinds to add natural light in; keeping the door open to the already awake sounds of the house; or cooking a favorite meal (in this house it's always the smell of bacon that pulls people out of slumber).

Watch Their TV Shows

Sit down and watch what they watch. It can be easy as our children grow up to be the one introducing new shows. To be in control of what is on the TV and slipping into other distractions when "their" shows are on. But when we engage, distraction-free, in something that our child is entertained by, we lift their hearts. It's like saying, through our actions, "Your interests matter too."

When I sit still and pay attention to what pulls them in, I get the chance to peek inside their brain, to understand what makes them laugh and to hear stories I would have otherwise missed had I walked away.

Happy memories are the leftovers of loving someone just a little bit more.

Let Them Be the DJ

Since my oldest son loves music, I gave up the DJ role pretty early on and left it to him. Whether it be choosing the radio station or building a playlist of favorite tunes on Spotify, giving up the DJ role invites me into his world to hear what he's been listening to lately. It fills him up with a sense of control as he spins up the tunes for us all to enjoy. Being a full member of the family means being able to display your choices all over the place so others can know you through what it is you love. This whole DJ business has been a beautiful way for that to unfold.

Tie Their Laces

When you are in a rush to get to playing with your friends, the last thing on your mind is learning how to tie your laces. With your years and years of experience, you are going to be way faster. And from their perspective, it's tough to focus on learning something new when you have a burning desire to be doing something else. The loving thing to do in that moment is to willingly bend down and tie their laces.

This idea can be extended to include a lot of the little things we can do for our children throughout their growing up. It can be easy to buy into the idea that children are being lazy by asking for our help. Or that at some magic age decided by someone outside of your child they should be able to do these things on their own, without hesitation. I am here to assure you that your twenty-five-year-old son or daughter will not be driving across town to ask you to tie their shoelaces.

Make Pancake Shapes

Pancakes are fun in general—sugary, gooey yumminess. Making pancakes into shapes that will make your little ones smile, adds a whole new dimension to the fun. I have made them a couple of different ways. Sometimes I take a metal cookie cutter and lay it right on the grill, place the pancake mix inside and let the magic reveal itself. For a more precise look, or if using a plastic cookie cutter, I would recommend cooking a full pancake and then cutting out the shape.

Whipped Cream

Whipped cream it! It's my favorite way to add a little extra magic to the day. Who doesn't love an extra dollop of whipped cream on their hot chocolate, strawberries, or ice cream? Use your imagination here; whipped cream tops many things.

Another fun thing is to turn the whipped cream your child's favorite color. Or the color of a special celebration, like pink for Valentine's or green for St. Patrick's. One super secret fun way is to invite your child to make the whipped cream with you and hide the food coloring. Dip it in the bowl before the cream or add a few drops on the mixer's paddle and watch with delight as your child is amazed by the magic color-changing whip cream.

Hot Dates

Oh, hot dates! They are all about taking time out to do something with your child that speaks to their heart. If you have more than one child, this can be that one on one time that fills you both up. It can be as simple as picnic lunch on the front lawn or as extravagant as a concert for two. Around here, I usually invite the child I am having the date with to choose what we will get up to. If they are stuck, I will seek out activities I know will spark their heart. Throw it on the calendar so that everyone knows it is coming up, then sit back and enjoy the marvelous memories you are making. A side bonus for us has been that since the boys understand the wonder of a hot date, they don't question why mom and dad need one from time to time.

Extra Bubbles in the Bath

There is this fabulous picture of my son, taken when he was around three years old, and the bubbles in his bathtub are taller than he is. We had just moved to a new home, the new tub had jets, and he turned them on during his bubble bath. A huge mountain of bubbles grew around him. Yes, it was a potential mess, but in that moment I saw the joy pouring out of him, and I knew this was far more important than any amount of bubbles or water I would later be mopping up. From that day forward we always added extra bubbles to the bath, for no other reason than the potential joy they have in them.

Pajama Days

I love me a good pajama day. Or heck, a week-long string of them. It may be true that the very first thing all four of us do when we walk in the door from being out in the world is strip down and dive into our coziest PJs. Permission to spend the day in pajamas invites a no pressure air of relaxation into the day. These sorts of moments invite connection and creativity into the child's world.

Random Acts of Kindness

We've all heard of them before, random acts of kindness: doing something completely unexpected for a total stranger. Apply that same thing to your child. Clean their room, pick up that game they've been saving for, or make them breakfast in bed. Build a bank of special memories, one unexpected act of kindness at a time.

Play Together

"Play in our species serves many valuable purposes. It is a means by which children develop their physical, intellectual, emotional, social, and moral capacities. It is a means of creating and preserving friendships. It also provides a state of mind that, in adults as well as children, is uniquely suited for high-level reasoning, insightful problem solving, and all sorts of creative endeavors."

~ Peter Gray

Entering into my child's world of play has been hands down the most effective way to keep our strong connection fueled. When the boys were younger, the play went on throughout the day, for hours on end. We were deep in imaginary worlds, exploring, adventuring, and creating original stories. It truly was magical.

It can be hard in an already busy life to find time for play. Especially for children like mine who would have loved to play with me one on one all day long. Some quick strategies for giving them or yourself time can be to agree to a game that has a definite start and end, to use a timer for the time you have available, or to pencil time together in on the calendar if you are busy when an invitation comes in. It is worth a quick mention that the time of their wanting to play vanishes in the blink of an eye. I now find myself being the one inviting people to play with me.

In the teen years, the invitations will look different. Strategies I have used are finding a cool YouTube video to share, a new app, a challenge to complete together and new board games. The moments when we play together are sweet memories in the making. Or as Peter says, the building of some pretty high-level reasoning, insightful, creative human beings!

Celebrate

Celebrate just because. Call them JUST BE-CAUSE DAYS, or just because cakes. Just celebrate. There are so many moments that pass quickly by us in this fast-paced world. In taking the time to pause and celebrate, we are helping our children notice the little bits of awesome that build a lifetime of joy. I think half-birthdays require, at the very least, a dance party in the kitchen. As does making it through an awkward conversation with a stranger that you had hoped to avoid. Chocolate bar toast indeed.

The how of the celebrating will mould the culture of your family, highlighting what's of value and importance to each of you. The constant reminder of how you do hard things will build the resilience required to be a happiness seeker in this world.

Let Them Plan Meals

Handing over the meal planning can take a rather large leap of faith depending on the age and stage you are at in your journey with children. The first steps might begin with an invitation to choose a meal in the upcoming week. The following week could find you with a sous chef. Finally, you might find yourself feet up on the couch waiting for dinner to arrive!

The brilliance for me of engaging the boys in meal planning was that it helped me to understand their current food preferences. It also upped the chances that everyone would eat the same meal. It created a sense of ownership around exploring new foods and more than once this happened: "Hey, mom. I saw this cool idea on Tasty. Can we make it?" Then there we were, a few days later, side by side in the kitchen building cooking skills and creating sweet, sweet memories.

Love Lists

Love lists are my most favorite way to express what I am seeing and loving about the people with whom I share space. It's simple and easy. Make a list of the things you love, in that moment, about your child and present it to them. It can come attached to breakfast, tucked under fresh laundry, or decorated and framed on their bedroom wall. It's a quick way to say, 'Hey, this is how I see you and love you in the world.'

Cut the Tags Out

I have a child who can not stand to have a tag on any part of his clothing.

He also struggled for years with the way that socks and shoes felt on his feet. One of the biggest love gifts we can give to our children is to listen to how these little things are bothering them and help to clear the path so they can get back to paying attention to the serious job of playing.

It can be hard for children who, by design, live in the now, to put aside feelings of irritation or discomfort. When we can listen and help clear the path for them, we can stop a larger meltdown from occurring. A simple snip, snip, and you have given them the gift of a day free of skin-prickling irritation.

Footwear falls under this category as well. I had a shoe closet full of shoes for my son and on any given day not one of them felt right. Not to mention the fact that I was also offering up socks to wear with these shoes. It took us a while to find the perfect shoes for winter (rubber boots) and summer (Crocs), and glory be when we located those seamless socks! In all this time together, troubleshooting, experimenting, listening, and trusting, I was sending an important message to my son, 'You matter.'

Fog Writing

Let them write in the fog that forms on the bathroom window after a hot shower or bath. Because one day you just might find yourself lying exhausted in a hot bath looking at a sweet message that reads "I love you mom," that has been hidden away, waiting for that exact moment.

Jump in Puddles

It takes only an extra second to stop on the way somewhere to jump in the puddles. Take the jump and see the wonder and surprise on your child's face. If wet footwear is an issue, you can also jump over the puddle. The idea is to take a split second to up the joy as you travel from one space to the next.

Smell the Roses

All the flowers, really. The idea again is just slow-ing down enough to notice the present moment and how it might be lifted. Our children are beautiful examples of noticing the world around them. I've experimented and can tell you that the time it takes to smell a rose matches the time it takes to tug a hand and insist we keep on rushing past. I bet you can guess which one results in a happier child.

Dessert First

Eat dessert first sometimes. I mean, in the larger scheme of life with your children, does it really matter that once in a while you eat the ice cream before the broccoli? I am pretty sure the chances of 'that time we ate ice cream for dinner' making the highlight reel are pretty high.

Awesome the Holidays

The holidays are a great way to add some awesome to our kids' lives. I know the big ones already come with all sorts of ways to celebrate. I am thinking about those smaller holidays. St. Patrick's Day in our house is often filled with green clothing, shamrock shakes, and a menacing visit from a leprechaun. Valentine's Day is kicked up a level when the milk's turned pink and the hidden drip of color on the whisk turns the pancakes red.

If you do a quick Google search, you will find that almost every day in the calendar year has a holiday attached to it. National Ice Cream Day, Pie Day, Eat a Donut Day, and the list goes on. Why not throw a few more holidays on your calendar? See what fabulous ideas your creative children come up with to show you how to amp up the awesome.

Strew and Spark

My children have taught me more about topics that would never have crossed my path than I could have imagined. When I am paying attention, I discover what is tugging at my children's interest. Then I get to gather up a collection of cool objects, books, and maybe even arrange a trip or two that just might expand their exploration. I might set up a space in our home like a museum exhibit for their latest interest.

The term I've heard used for this laying about of cool items is strewing. Sometimes what I lay out sparks an adventure I could have never imagined! Technology is great for this as well because I can text articles, images, GIFs, and more to my people that they can engage with at their leisure.

Here's a few ideas I've seen used brilliantly. A well-placed stack of books or magazines in the bathroom. Found objects gathered on a living room table with a magnifying glass. Toys set up that invite curious minds into play—like the beginning of a Lego building. These tiny moments of strewing things throughout the house that might spark play, joy, or conversation, are some of my favorite memories.

Tell Sweet Stories

I am a storyteller. I love to spin a grand tale. I love to get to know people through their stories, and this is something that has become a cherished part of my life with my boys. I always know they are making deep friendships when they begin spinning our most favorite yarns with people we have just met. They are telling the tales of who we are in the world and highlighting the moments that have defined us.

I think it can be easy when getting together with groups of other parents to tell the sorts of stories about our children that highlight what we are struggling with. Those stories do not convey a message of love. They do not show our children that they truly are the hero of their own story. When we share the stories that show their growth, their strength, and the wonderful memories we are building together, we are creating strength of character. We are giving our children access back into moments in their childhood. They are our living oral history that will continue to be handed down for years to come.

My boys lost both their grandfathers early on in their journey. These men live on through the stories we tell about them over and over again. I hear them quoted by my boys in ways that show how, after death, they have lived on. Story allows us to explain the hard parts of life in a way that is digestible by young minds.

Consent

I think it is important to touch on the subject of consent. Touch without consent is a huge NO, in our house. Our children are human beings whose consent is required when it comes to their bodies. It is up to me to model and respect that in our relationship so that my children have the skills to do that in all the relationships they will be in throughout their lifetime. That is why it has never been a requirement for my children to hug, kiss or shake hands with anyone they don't want to. It is why I am happy to step between a well-meaning relative and my child if I can see that their boundary is not being respected. Children are human beings and deserve the same respect as any other person. Get consent first.

Part of consent falls under bodily autonomy as well. When my child is certain they dislike a food, I listen. The food is digesting inside their body, not mine. How can I know better? As well, listening to and respecting a child's choice about their body keeps their intuition awake. It shows them the value of knowing their own body so they will feel empowered to listen to it throughout their lifetime.

Massage

Whether it's a short shoulder rub or an extended back massage, massage is a great way to connect with our children. Essential oils on the feet of someone feeling rundown help kick up the immune system, from both the benefits of touch and the oils soaking in. A quick 'tickle back,' as we call it, can bring a moment of closeness to a busy day. Sitting in silence with an offer for a hand massage can help work through challenging moments in the business of growing up. Massage has often been my way into reconnection when life has been busy. I know that, for my boys, sometimes reconnecting starts better without words and this too has given us a great way to do that.

Wrestle

Wrestling! That was a big part of our lives. We set some guidelines ahead of time: a word that we all knew meant stop; which moves were considered illegal; and then we renegotiated along the way. It was a super fun way to get some energy out while rolling around with each other. I know the boys still enjoy a good, healthy wrestling match with one another.

Cuddles

Cuddles are my favorite way of staying connected. I tend to be that mom who jumps into bed with each of my children when they first wake up to kick the day off on a good and connected note. And hugs, so many hugs. They are a great way to get up and close in each other's space.

With the teen years upon us and people sometimes needing more space, things can look different, but keeping connected through touch is still important. Some ways I do this include sitting knee to knee or elbow to elbow on the couch. Maybe an invitation to hold hands while walking down the street, or an arm around a shoulder during a particularly challenging moment.

I will say it again because of its importance: consent is essential. Sometimes consent is withdrawn based on where our children are at present. Verbal check-ins are important, and so is reading non-verbal cues. A child who pulls away wants space. One who leans in might not. When in doubt, ask. Make sure you are continuing to respect the boundaries that are evolving in your child's healthy development of self.

Bold Handhold

The bold handhold in a public place. Worth a try, right? I can handle the rejection of a dropped hand but cannot live without those moments when it stays clasped inside of mine. I've been known to slip my hand in when walking through the mall or down the street. I will take whatever reaction comes. Sometimes it's a tight hold and a quick release. Other times we linger, hooked at the fingers for the entire walk. It's all those tiny moments that hold us together!

Make the Damn Tuna Melt

I heard a talk one day at a conference, and the title was, "Make the Damn Tuna Melt." The basic idea is, you're exhausted, it's been a long day, you've packed it in and are headed to bed when you are met by your child in the hallway with a request. "Can you make me a tuna melt?"

I know my first reaction, and often the one I end with is, "Make your own damn tuna melt." To which your child, if they are as committed as the speaker's, will respond with "But yours are so much better." It would be easy right now to think my child is simply trying to pull one over on me. To guilt me into making them some food. I think it is likely just as true that my child is saying, "I would like a little bit of your love right now." When I hear that message, a whole different response spills out of my heart.

Our children will come to us and need us and want us in a whole host of different ways through-out their growing up. I am realizing that this will often come at what may feel like, to my grown-up brain, the worst possible time. If we "just make the damn tuna melt," our actions speak straight to the heart of our child. Whether they were simply hungry, feeling tired themselves, or wanting a little extra love, we showed up, we filled their bucket.

LOVE IN
PRESENCE

Say YES as Much as Possible

Building magical childhoods involves saying yes as much as possible. Other examples of saying yes include: "maybe later," "let's explore that a little further," "we can save up for that," "let's research other ways." You get my drift.

Sometimes your child will come to you with the wildest, craziest ideas.

And you know in your heart, or adult experience, that it is impossible. However, if you say yes, you are teaming up with your child to go on this wild and crazy adventure. At some point along the way, your child will naturally conclude that this idea just cannot find its way to coming true. They will own all of that learning and you will be seen forever in their eyes as the cheerleader that is on board for chasing down their wildest, craziest dreams.

Greet with Excitement

When you see your child, greet them enthusiastically. See all the love that you have wound up in your heart and unleash it on them. Each morning I am genuinely excited to see my boys stumble from their slumber and I bubble over with enthusiasm in my "good morning." Because when you strip it all back, I am absolutely thrilled that they woke up and we have another day to be side by side in this world.

Let Them Be the Expert

Let the child be the expert! This, I think, can be hard for us adults to do. I mean, we worked hard to get the information that we have, and we like to share it with our children.

When we allow our children to be the expert on a topic and sit in the role of learner, we create a great space for their expertise to grow because learning deepens when we teach what we know to another person. And when we embody curiosity, we can help bring out our children's curiosity. "How do you know that?" said with curiosity can begin a wild afternoon of information exploration. Simply telling a child something may not lead to greater understanding if they don't have a hook to hang the knowledge on. Leading with a question that hands the learning back helps build the hook and solidify that information. Put on the hat of the curious one turning to the experts, your children, and enjoy where they take you.

Time IN

We all know what a time out is. It's recommended all over the place. Isolate a child when they have done something wrong. Make them feel bad in hopes that they never do that again.

If our goal is to stay connected, what if we turn that around and do a time IN. Children who are making, big loud noises, whether literally or figuratively through their behaviors, actually need more love. If someone needs more love and you don't give it to them, all you are doing is keeping the bucket empty. Instead, we can try to fill that bucket. Have a time in, hold a hand, listen to a tantrum, offer a hug, or simply sit nearby until the storm passes and a conversation can be had.

Hold Space

Simply occupying the same space as my child without words, without having to fix anything, is a beautiful gift. There is a way of sitting with someone that conveys, 'I am here for you without judgement,' in a way that words simply cannot do.

Different from a time in, holding space does not always have to be during a time of frustration. It can also come at a time of joy, or just as a reminder that a child is not alone in the world. I have a son who is quiet with his feelings and process. Often I will sit at the foot of his bed and just hold space. I have often thought it didn't matter to him whether I was there or not but then I would get up to go he would say, "Mom, don't go." He needed me to be quietly sitting and holding space for reasons I may never know, but that definitely convey love for him.

Listen More

Thich Nhat Hanh describes a sort of listening called compassionate (or deep) listening. He says, "Deep listening is the kind of listening that can help relieve the suffering of the other person."

It is hard to be a child in our world. They are shushed, made fun of, ignored, and, in general, treated as less than full human beings. It is also a big job to live in a body that is always growing and changing; as the mind expands to understand things wider and farther away from yourself. As their mom, the greatest gift I can give is this idea of deep listening. Of simply sitting with them to hear their suffering.

I know for myself the hardest part is to clamp down on my tongue.

Because there are times when the words that are coming my way feel untrue. They are not how I saw the situation. That is not how I would retell the story. However, think of a time when your heart was bursting over with emotion, heartbreak, or wrongdoing, and someone dismissed all of that as a misunderstanding. It doesn't feel good.

To quote some more from Thich Nhat Hanh, "You listen with only one purpose, help him or her empty his heart." That is how I wish and strive to listen to my child each time. Whether it be something that is an upset or a celebration, I wish to sit and listen with them while they empty their heart.

Power With

"To trust children we must first learn to trust ourselves ... and most of us were taught as children that we could not be trusted."

~ John Holt

Drink that in for a moment. Most of us were shown as children that we could not be trusted and that adults held all the power. So, now to be standing by our children it's easier to slip into, "Do as I say, I am the adult here," because switching it up means we have to do the hard, internal work of shifting our own experience.

When my son was four years old, he wrote his name across the hood of our car in permanent marker. There were a lot of thoughts that ran through my mind when I first encountered this. Most of them included punishment and power over to make sure he never did that again because he had, in my mind, in that moment, ruined our car.

A few deep breaths later I started to have a conversation with him. "Dude we aren't supposed to use permanent markers on the car. I don't think I can get it off and someday we might want to sell the car. Let's see if we can find a way to get that off." Hand in hand we made our way to the computer to search for ways to get permanent marker off the hood of a car. Turns out you can use toothpaste to do such a thing, which he thought was pretty cool. "Shall we see if it works?" Of course, at four, the idea of squirting large amounts of toothpaste on the car was a fun idea. So we did it, and it worked! Together we found a solution, together we fixed the car, and together we learned something new that's come in handy more than once. But most importantly, our relationship was kept intact.

Admit When You're Wrong

Not a single one of us is perfect. Not a single one of us knows everything. And not a single one of us is getting through this life without making a whole lot of mistakes. Admitting you are wrong to your children when you make a mistake or get a fact wrong goes a long way to sharing the power.

I don't know about you, but I like to be right. However, this journey of parenting has really humbled me. The world of the Internet means my children often come across information that runs counter to what I know to be true. And sometimes I am dead wrong about the things I thought to be true. Engaging from the place of "Wow, I had no idea. How did you figure that out?" opens the door to conversations that can expand on knowledge, redirect understanding, and open minds.

Trust Their Boundaries

Our children are going to test out the idea of setting boundaries on us first. I know that many believe that children learn about boundaries through having parents with firm boundaries. I'm gonna challenge that idea and suggest that one way to support our children in setting healthy boundaries is to respect the ones they start out setting with us.

It can be easy to overlook the boundaries set by our children and step all over them without even really noticing. I remember the first time my son told me he did not like quinoa—a food he had been eating for years. My knee jerk reaction was to say, "Of course you do, you have been eating that for years now." Something in him felt a need to set this line for himself. So, I lovingly saddle up beside him and say, "Alright. I'll try and remember that next time." He may change his mind the next day, or the next minute. My role is not to throw back in his face that he keeps changing his mind about things, but to meet him in the moment that he is in and respect the boundaries he is putting in place.

Some folks may jump in here and say I am catering to his every whim or making myself crazy by adjusting meal plans. I'm going to counter that I am just listening to another human being and helping them figure out what they do and do not like in the world and trusting the process. Heck, my husband changes his mind near as often as my children and I am not all up in his face forcing him to eat a food that doesn't feel right in his mouth for whatever reason.

By supporting my children as they discover what feels right for them, I am setting them up for a lifetime of not only setting healthy boundaries for themselves but also in knowing boundaries are something to be respected.

A Sense of Belonging

Our opportunity here is to be at the center of our children's moral compass as they head out into the wider world. This does not mean they will not challenge our beliefs or will hold the same opinions. It means that when making hard decisions they will rely on our unwavering support.

When we explore our family history through story, we give our children a deeper sense of belonging. It is through these stories that our children have an opportunity to experience themselves in relationship with others.

When we give voice to our children, through personal choices as well as family decisions, we show them the important role they hold within the family unit. We bolster their sense of belonging, and they can see themselves on the timeline of value and importance within the family unit.

It is this strong sense of belonging that allows our children to head out into the world knowing they will always have a place where they belong. That's the sort of confidence that lets a person reach for their wildest dreams.

Use Positive Language

Words matter. We are creating the voice that is developing inside of our child's mind. The one that talks to them in their moments of struggle. I want that voice to whisper nothing but compassion and encouragement. This starts with the language I choose to use with them.

It can be as simple as turning statements into actions for the child. For example, "Don't run." does not give a child an action whereas "Walk please." conveys something they can do. Or simply "Stop!" for more urgent situations.

We can better help our children understand their world when we move away from "Be careful." to "Notice how slippery the ground is under your feet." We can help them recognize danger by changing "Don't play over there." into "Did you notice there are rusty nails sticking out of that fence post?" This helps our children survey an area and lean into their own sense of safety rather than relying on us to police their environment.

This also applies to making sure we do not pose a

question when there is not a choice in a situation. The most common example of this is asking "Do you want a sibling?" right before announcing a pregnancy. Some children will answer no and be quite upset that the sibling is showing up anyway. Another example is, "Do you want to brush your teeth?" when we already know it's a must do in our house. Instead, try "Would you like the pink toothbrush or blue one? Or "Am I brushing your teeth tonight or are you?" The idea is to set everyone up for connection instead of struggle.

Finally, messages in moments of frustration are opportunities to build that voice I was speaking of earlier. "I can see you are frustrated." instead of "You are frustrating me." "I need ten minutes to finish this job." as opposed to "Stop bothering me." The goal is to turn the statement into kindness and help build a vocabulary our children can use through life's rough seas.

Family Mission Statement

When the boys were young, we decided to make a family mission statement. If memory serves me, the boys were about three and five at the time. We sat down together, the four of us, and discussed how we all wanted to feel in the family, things people could do to help with that, and what we wanted to be as a family together. It was playful, as the boys were young. I captured the keywords that truly resonated with each one of us.

Including the boys in the process was crucial. It conveyed to them that they are essential members of our family and that what they desire to feel and have in our family is as important as what their dad and I want. This was not a list of rules we were putting on to our children. Together, we were designing an anchor for future discussions and decisions. When the seas got rough, we could come back to this.

In the end, we decided our family statement was "To unite in our commitment to love one another unconditionally." I put the words in glitter glue on a piece of canvas that has made every move with us, hanging in a prominent place in our home, as a reminder to us all of what it is we are doing as this unit. This statement has given some structure to how we decide to treat each other, how we decide to spend our time, and how we genuinely engage as a family.

Shift Your Irritation

I am easily irritated. By sounds, by touches, by over stimulation. There is no logic to my irritation—it's just a part of being me in the world. I do have some control over how I react to my irritation, though, and who I toss that stuff on to. Because I am home full time with the boys, it can be easy—and happens more then I would like—to hand them the brunt of an irritated moment that had ABSOLUTELY nothing to do with them.

I am committed to loving better, so I try to protect them from my irritation bombs. When children are young and in the ego-centric phase of life, it's tough to understand that something isn't about you. That's when I had to work the hardest at walking away, taking deep breaths, and apologizing.

As the boys have gotten older, I can express my irritation verbally now in such a way that they don't take it on. "I'm super irritated right now. Can you ask me again in ten minutes?" as one example. This shift allows me time to re-center to my intention as their mom as opposed to reacting to the circumstance.

Sleep Happens

Oh, sleep. Sweet, sweet sleep. Be it yours or be it theirs, it is the golden moment many parents seek in a day. Before I had my boys, a short night's sleep was eight hours—the norm was closer to ten. Becoming a mother stole that right out from underneath me without warning. I fought long and hard with myself and my children in the early years in search of that sleep-filled wonderland. All that happened was a lot of tears, frustration, and downright anger.

Sleep does happen. The more relaxed we are about it, the better it can be for everyone involved. I was that mom who pulled her babies into bed with her because I wasn't willing to give up the extra sleep time it would take to gather them from a separate bed for nursing—rolling over saved time and effort. I applied that filter quickly to many moments throughout our sleeping. My husband and I would remind each other regularly that the goal is for each person to get as much sleep as possible. Not that we meet some arbitrary idea of what was "normal."

I've recorded myself telling bedtimes stories for the boy who can't fall asleep without hearing my voice. I've purchased noise cancelling headphones for the one who wants to stay up later than everyone else but can't bear to be alone in the house. It was about finding solutions that allowed all four people to fall asleep peacefully and get the most sleep possible.

I know we looked weird to many people throughout the different phases. I assure you now with teenagers in the house each person falls asleep on their own, in their own room, including my husband and I because he snores and I want to sleep.

Relax. Make bedtime a fun connection time and see how much more rested you all become.

Know Their Friends

Being connected with my children's friends is quite possibly the most amazing gift my children have given me. Why do I put this down as a way to love more when it comes to our children? Because the non-verbal part of this says, "Hey, I like the people you hang out with and your relationships matter to me."

It can be easy to slip into the more traditional forms of friendship that look like all the parents gathered in one room while the children connect and play in the other. I know there have been times throughout this journey where that has been the exact magic that has filled my draining cup. At the same time, I encourage each of you to step away from the parent table from time to time and connect with the children.

When I know the child that my child is struggling with, I can often offer up a perspective that comes from love and understanding, as opposed to blame, during a conflict. I can see both sides of the equation and offer up buckets of compassion for both parties, each of whom is desperate to feel heard and understood. From there, this can sometimes lead to the sort of resolution that keeps a friendship intact and sends my child off with another notch in their problem-solving tool kit.

Work on Your Issues

I could write an entire book about working on your issues, however, I just wanted to pop in here and add this to the list of ways you can love your children more. If you can clean up the things that are holding your heart shut, you will be better able to meet your child in this moment and love them from that place.

It's important to note that working on your issues happens away from your child. And it can take a whole lot of different forms. I'm no expert on the how to part of this; but I can share a few things that work for me: building community; reading about parenting from a peaceful, connected place; breathing; journaling; and the occasional therapy session. The end result of a healed heart is a stronger ability to find joy in every day with my children.

It's certainly not an easy task especially, when, as a parent of young children, you already feel like you are burning a very short candle on both ends. When the boys were super little, breathing was about the only thing I could pull off between all of their needs. My mantra, when I was sure the world was falling apart and that I was in need of some serious help was, "You are just tired." Back then I had to remind myself, some days on an hourly basis, that really, I was just tired, more than tired I was exhausted.

But as the fog of having young children began to lift, there were short moments when I had a little oxygen for myself. Time to start pulling apart my triggers, locating their proper source, and making my way toward healing them.

I cannot in good faith close out this section without including a piece about taking all the kindness and compassion and unconditional love we have for our children and dolloping that stuff all over ourselves liberally on a super, duper regular basis.

"What you do for yourself—any gesture of kindness, any gesture of gentleness, any gesture of honest and clear seeing toward yourself, will affect how you experience your world. In fact, it will transform how you experience the world."

~ from Pema Chödrön's book,
Comfortable with Uncertainty

Walk Your Talk

There is that saying we've all heard before: "Actions speak louder than words," and this is also true of this dance of parenting. Hearing "I love you" before receiving a spanking does not make the spanking hurt any less.

If our actions are saying something opposite to our well-intentioned words, our child will become deaf to the hollow words and hear only what our actions are saying.

This extends beyond parenting to include the human being we are in the world. If I am at home telling my children that we are all born equal and all deserve to be treated equally and then I turn a blind eye to discrimination that happens right in front of me, my actions are telling my child it's okay to discriminate. If I sit at home and tell my children that homelessness is a problem in our neighborhood and then I pretend the man with his outstretched hand is invisible on the street corner, I am negating the message. I am not saying I have to put something in that man's hand every time, or end homelessness, but I do feel I have a responsibility to meet that person eye to eye and acknowledge that they are in the world alongside me.

Taking action beyond our words gives our children a framework from which to act themselves.

Tell the Truth

This one trips me up over and over, and I don't know if it is human nature or about how I came to understand the world around me. As an adult, it can feel easier to make up little white lies than to face the meltdown or disappointment that might come from the truth.

Now, before I continue, I want to make a clear distinction between telling the truth and over-whelming our children with devastating events that are happening in the world. What I am referring to here is maintaining truth in the re-lationship with your child—the little day to day truths about things like whether or not there is ice cream in the freezer. Perhaps it might feel easier to say there is not any ice cream in the house than to have another discussion about whether or not ice cream for dinner is appropriate. What hap-pens, though, is we weave a weaker foundation in the way our child trusts us. I want my children to trust me, so I choose the honest route, even when it's the harder route in the moment.

Lying by choice is harder to forgive than telling the truth about accidents that happen. They would much rather I tell the truth and maintain the integrity of our relationship. I also want to show them that owning up to your mistakes in a relationship is much easier then muddying the waters with half-truths and stories that you have to remember at a later date. I want them to tell me the truth about the dent in the car and deal with my initial overreactions than try and hide it all with a big fat lie that will make untangling the details that much harder for all of us. I want them to know it's okay to make mistakes, own them, and carry on. I want to communicate love by offering them the truth at every turn in the road.

Be Their Friend

I know there is a lot of controversy in the world about being our children's friends. How we are supposed to be the parent, not the friend. One quote states, "Your child does not need a forty-year-old friend." I'm going to say, "Yes they do." Go ahead and be your child's friend. Let's take a look at the definition of a friend.

1. a friend: one attached to another by affection or esteem

I think that's a pretty great way to be in relationship with your child. Of course, you being your child's friend is not going to look the same as the friends they have in their peer group because they have different affections that attach them. I want to earn the esteemed title of friend in my child's eyes. I want to show them respect, stand by them through the tough times, be the person they lean on, listen without judgement, and be attached by affection. Because my now young child is stepping closer to the doorstep of adulthood every day, and when they walk through, I'm going to make damn sure they do so wanting to remain friends with me for life.

Parent with Intention

Am I parenting from a place of intention or as a reaction to the set of circumstances that are in front of me? Yesterday I found my son head down on his desk in front of his Xbox, tears hanging on his words. I asked what was up. He started to yell and point and say things that did not compute for me. I reacted from a place of circumstance and met his angry words with just as much frustration as he was feeling. We were both wound up in the fury of miscommunication, hurling useless information at one another and spiraling further and further away from any sort of solution.

In a breath, I found my way back to intention. My intention as a mother is to hold the space of peace for my children when the world around them gets wobbly, and they can't figure out which way is up. I want to be their constant, their support, their unconditional place. That looks like a lot less talking and way more listening and patience. Solutions rarely arrive in the heat of the storm. They more often show up in the calm that comes after. I want my actions to repeat, "You, my dear child, are much more important than any stress ball that may tumble between us. Your sense of self means more than any moment of frustration that might push us to the edges of our anger. Our relationship matters to me, more than mistakes and misunderstanding. Yes, my child, this unconditional love is yours to have in your weakest and your strongest moments."

Trust Their Learning

I like to think I know more because I am older, but the truth is, these humans we are sharing space with often tap into wisdom that has yet to cross our path. My children don't learn the same way that I learn. When I step in between them and what they are exploring, I can interrupt the natural talents that lead them to a particular exploration. My oldest son is a musician—he's only ever had two paid lessons, yet he can play a collection of instruments. I tried to force my agenda and could see him pull away from his passion. So, instead, I became his most adored fan and watched as he built his own lessons and excelled. When we can sit back and trust in our children's learning, we see their talents flourish. This trust also gifts our child with a lifelong passion and deeper trust in their own ability to learn.

See the Child, Not the Behavior

Focus on your child, not their behavior. I know this is million times easier said than done. Yet, when we can see the child asking for help behind the screaming tantrum in the store, we are more able to move toward support. When I came in butting heads with the behavior I was hoping to eradicate, it took much longer to resolve than those where I saw my sweet child.

I have sat down in the middle of a store to sooth the child who can't decide which shiny object to bring home. I've scooped a lanky six-year-old into my arms and rocked him like his baby self when the sand in his eyes was more than he could handle. When we can see the child, we can locate the need. When the need is met, we can move on in a faster and more loving way.

MOVING FORWARD

This is a short list that I have started here.

At the end of the book, you will find some empty pages for you to take it from here! Lean into your own wisdom as a parent and spill out your unique list of ways to show up with joy and love in your children's lives. You are, after all, the most quali-fied expert on the child you are raising.

Listen to your heart and find your way through.

I trust in the magic you are about to uncover as a partner in love with your child.

MY IDEAS